Hydrogen Fuel

by Barbara J. Davis

**Science and Curriculum Consultant:
Debra Voege, M.A.,
Science Curriculum Resource Teacher**

CHELSEA CLUBHOUSE

An Imprint of Chelsea House Publishers

Energy Today: Hydrogen Fuel

Chelsea Clubhouse
An imprint of Chelsea House Publishers
132 West 31st Street
New York NY 10001

Library of Congress Cataloging-in-Publication Data
Davis, Barbara J., 1952-
  Hydrogen fuel / by Barbara J. Davis.
    p. cm. — (Energy today)
  Includes bibliographical references and index.
  ISBN 978-1-60413-783-5
  1. Hydrogen as fuel—Juvenile literature. I. Title. II. Series.
  TP359.H8D38 2010
  665.8'1—dc22   2009043388

Chelsea Clubhouse books are available at special discounts when purchased in bulk quantities for businesses, associations, institutions, or sales promotions. Please call our Special Sales Department in New York at (212) 967-8800 or (800) 322-8755.

You can find Chelsea Clubhouse on the World Wide Web at http://www.chelseahouse.com

Developed for Chelsea House by RJF Publishing LLC (www.RJFpublishing.com)
Project Editor: Jacqueline Laks Gorman
Text and cover design by Tammy West/Westgraphix LLC
Illustrations by Spectrum Creative Inc.
Photo research by Edward A. Thomas
Index by Nila Glikin
Composition by Westgraphix LLC
Cover printed by Bang Printing, Brainerd, MN
Book printed and bound by Bang Printing, Brainerd, MN
Date printed: May 2010
Printed in the United States of America

Photo Credits: 5: NASA; 6: AP Images; 8: Library of Congress LC-DIG-ppmsca-02439; 9: Image Source/Photolibrary; 11: AP Images; 15: (top) Vasilyev/Shutterstock; 18: Warren Gretz/NREL; 19: © Grant Heilman Photography/Alamy; 23: Rich Bain/NREL; 25: Matt Stiveson/NREL; 27: KIM SHIFLETT/Reuters/Landov; 31: (top) YURIKO NAKAO/Reuters/Landov, (bottom) AP Images; 33: iStockphoto; 34: © Roger Ressmeyer/CORBIS; 36: Peter Bennett/Ambient Images/Photolibrary; 39: Warren Gretz/NREL; 40: PAT GREENHOUSE/Boston Globe/Landov; 41: (top) AP Images, (bottom) Jianping Yu/NREL.

10 9 8 7 6 5 4 3 2 1

TABLE OF CONTENTS

Words that are defined in the Glossary are in **bold**
type the first time they appear in the text.

CHAPTER 1

What Is Hydrogen Fuel?

Our modern world relies on many different types of energy. We use electricity to light our homes and businesses. Heat energy warms us when the outside temperatures drop. Energy from oil (also called petroleum) runs the engines that move cars, planes, and boats. The energy demands of the future will be even greater than they are today. Where will that energy come from? **Hydrogen fuel** is one exciting possibility.

Hydrogen fuel is a material that is made of the **element** hydrogen. In its natural state, hydrogen is a colorless and odorless gas. Hydrogen gas has been used for many years as a raw material in the food, chemical, and oil refinery industries. For example, you may have noticed the term "hydrogenated oil" on a food label. The food industry uses hydrogen gas, in a process called hydrogenation, to turn liquid fats into solid fats. This makes the fats easier to use in food products. Store-bought cookies, for example, are often made with hydrogenated fats. These hydrogenated fats help the different ingredients in the cookies to hold together. Otherwise, the cookies would be too soft and runny to eat.

Hydrogen is also used in a number of other ways in the production of various foods. In addition, hydrogen is used to make products such as metal, glass, and ammonia, which is used in the making of fertilizer.

Carrying Energy

Hydrogen can also be used as a fuel carrier, or energy carrier. An energy carrier is a substance that moves energy in a usable form from one place to another.

As a fuel, the hydrogen is used in the form of a gas or liquid. It is called a secondary energy source because another form of energy is needed to produce the hydrogen fuel. The other form of energy is a primary energy source, such as natural gas, water, coal, or oil. These energy sources go through different types of processes that allow hydrogen fuel to be made. Electricity is another common example of an energy carrier and secondary energy source. It, too, requires the use of some other type of energy

During the 2008 Hydrogen Road Tour, hydrogen-powered cars traveled the roads of 18 states.

to produce it. For example, coal (the primary energy source) is burned in **power plants** to make electricity that is then carried over power lines to homes and businesses, where it is used.

Using Hydrogen Today

The National Aeronautics and Space Administration (NASA) currently uses most of the hydrogen fuel produced in the United States. NASA has used liquid hydrogen fuel since the 1970s to power the space shuttle rockets. Liquid hydrogen fuel is an energy-dense fuel. This means that if you compare gasoline and liquid hydrogen of equal **mass**, the liquid hydrogen will have three times the amount of energy as the gasoline. This surely helps when engineers are trying to push tons of steel off a rocket launch pad!

Car manufacturers have designed several types of hydrogen-powered vehicles. For the most part, these vehicles are not yet ready for the public, but they are getting close. Honda,

Mercedes-Benz, and Toyota are among the car manufacturers that have developed a number of hydrogen-fueled concept cars and **prototypes**. These cars may end up in your local car dealership before too long.

Drawbacks to Hydrogen Fuel

Hydrogen fuel is difficult to make and store. Liquid hydrogen has to be kept very cold, at a temperature of –423.17° Fahrenheit (–252.87° Celsius)! This requires special insulated storage tanks that are large and heavy. Making hydrogen gas into liquid hydrogen is a long process. The gas is placed in large tanks, then pressurized and cooled. These steps take a great deal of energy—especially electricity. In the end, about 40 percent of the energy that the liquid hydrogen can produce is "lost" because of the amount of electricity and other types

Did You Know?
A Vision of the Future

Jules Verne was a French author who wrote science fiction stories such as *Twenty Thousand Leagues Under the Sea* and *Around the World in Eighty Days*. In his 1874 book *The Mysterious Island*, Verne suggested the possibility that hydrogen could be used for fuel. He wrote, "I believe that water will one day serve as our fuel, that the hydrogen and oxygen which compose it, used alone or together, will supply an inexhaustible source of heat and light, burning with an intensity that coal cannot equal."

JACQUES ALEXANDRE CÉSAR CHARLES

Jacques Alexandre César Charles was born in France in 1746. He was a scientist who developed many inventions. He is especially remembered for something he did on August 27, 1783. That day, Charles launched an enormous balloon that was made of silk that had been coated with varnish. The balloon was filled with hydrogen gas. When the ropes holding the floating balloon were cut, it slowly ascended (rose) into the air. The balloon reached almost 3,000 feet (914 meters) before it landed just outside Paris, France. Unfortunately, the French peasants did not know what to make of the balloon as it came to the ground. They destroyed the balloon, thinking it was something evil.

Charles built another balloon. Then, on December 1, 1783, he and another man rode in the balloon, which ascended to a height of 1,800 feet (549 meters). It was the first time that human beings had ever used hydrogen to get from one place to another. Charles died in Paris in 1823.

Jacques Alexandre César Charles and a friend in Charles's hydrogen balloon, in 1783.

Hydrogen fuel must be stored in large, heavy tanks.

of energy needed to make and store the fuel. This means that there is a "cost" in energy to make the liquid hydrogen in the first place. The cost is the energy that is needed during the process of making liquid hydrogen.

The process to make and store liquid hydrogen prevents the fuel from being a good choice for everyday use. Imagine how hard it would be to carry around big liquid hydrogen tanks on your family car! Despite these problems, scientists are looking very closely at ways in which different forms of hydrogen fuel can be used.

Future Uses of Hydrogen Fuel

New research is showing that hydrogen fuel may be particularly valuable as a safe and clean way to produce the huge amount

In Their Own Words

"Someday we will run out of fossil fuels and perhaps more importantly, someday the environmental impact of these fuels will catch up with us. Global warming is a real threat, but fossil fuel combustion [burning] also causes local pollution. We need to stop burning things as much as possible"

Bruce Rittman, Center for Environmental Biotechnology, Biodesign Institute, Arizona State University

of electricity people use every day. Hydrogen fuel is also being looked at as an alternative to the gasoline we use to power vehicles large and small.

Most of the electricity used in cities and towns today is produced in power plants that burn **fossil fuels**—such as coal and natural gas—to generate the electricity. The oil that is **refined** to become gasoline is also a fossil fuel. In the future, hydrogen may serve as the energy for both electricity and vehicle power.

The Need for Alternatives

Why do we need alternatives to fossil fuels? There are a number of reasons. Fossil fuels are **nonrenewable** resources. They took millions of years to form, and there is only a limited supply of them on Earth. Once we use up the supply that currently exists, there will be no new fossil fuels to replace them. Eventually, they will be gone—and that time is not far off. The population of the United States (and the rest of the world) is growing. People are using more and more nonrenewable resources for energy. The world's supply of coal may run out

Did You Know?

The *Hindenburg* Disaster

The *Hindenburg* was a German airship—a craft with a rigid (stiff) frame. Inside was a large balloon filled with hydrogen gas, which caused the ship to lift up. Airships with balloons filled with hydrogen first flew in the 1850s, and they had become relatively common by the 1930s. In 1937, however, disaster struck during a flight of the *Hindenburg*, which was the world's largest airship. The airship burst into flames and exploded while landing in Lakehurst, New Jersey, killing 36 people. It was long thought that the hydrogen gas in the balloon had caught on fire. Recently, though, some scientists have said that a spark from lightning may have caused the airship's covering to catch on fire, so hydrogen was not responsible for the explosion.

The *Hindenburg*, traveling from Germany to New Jersey, burst into flames and exploded as it neared its landing field.

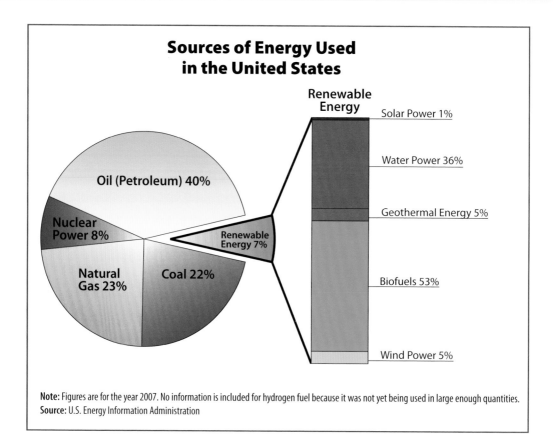

Sources of Energy Used in the United States

Oil (Petroleum) 40%

Nuclear Power 8%

Natural Gas 23%

Coal 22%

Renewable Energy 7%

Renewable Energy

Solar Power 1%

Water Power 36%

Geothermal Energy 5%

Biofuels 53%

Wind Power 5%

Note: Figures are for the year 2007. No information is included for hydrogen fuel because it was not yet being used in large enough quantities.
Source: U.S. Energy Information Administration

in 130 years. Natural gas may run out in about 60 years, and oil may run out in as little as 40 years. Other sources must be found to at least partly replace fossil fuels.

Burning fossil fuels also adds pollution to the air we breathe. The pollutants (harmful substances) can cause headaches and breathing problems, such as asthma. Burning fossil fuels also creates **acid rain**, which can harm rivers and lakes, plants and animals, and even buildings. In addition, fossil fuels have been linked to **global warming**. This is the gradual warming of Earth's climate, caused by the buildup of **carbon dioxide** and certain other gases in the **atmosphere**. Global warming has been linked to a melting of ice in Earth's polar regions and, therefore, to a rise in sea levels around the world. For the many cities built on the shores of the seas and in low-lying areas, an increase in water level poses a real threat.

It is not realistic to expect that people will need less energy in the future than they need now. So, something must be done. Scientists are looking for sources of energy that are plentiful and will not harm the environment. They are looking for **renewable** resources. There is a constant supply of these resources, or they can be made quickly. Sun, water, and wind are examples of renewable resources. They can all be used to produce electricity with little or no harm to the environment. Hydrogen fuel is seen as

In Their Own Words

"While hydrogen-fueled cars already exist, there are significant technical and economic barriers that must be overcome before we can put a hydrogen car in every American garage....When... advances are made, hydrogen can fill critical energy needs beyond transportation. Hydrogen can also be used to heat and generate electricity. The future possibilities of this energy source are huge."

U.S. Representative
Daniel Lipinski of Illinois

a constantly renewable source of energy as well. It is very likely that some day, hydrogen fuel might be used to produce electricity on the large scale needed to provide power for homes and businesses. It can also be used to produce smaller amounts of electricity that can be used as a source of energy to power transportation vehicles like cars, buses, and planes. The challenge is to find ways to use hydrogen fuel differently than it has been used in the past.

CHAPTER 2

How Is Hydrogen Fuel Made?

All matter is made of tiny bits called **atoms**. An atom is the smallest unit of an element that has the chemical properties (traits) of the element. Elements are the building blocks of matter in the universe. Elements combine with other elements to form different types of matter.

Hydrogen fuel is made with the element hydrogen. It is the most plentiful element in the universe. About 90 percent of the atoms in the universe are hydrogen atoms. It is the material that most stars—including our Sun—use to make energy.

Hydrogen Compounds

Hydrogen is a very light gas—even lighter than air. Because of this, it rises up in the atmosphere. Hydrogen atoms are not found by themselves on Earth. Instead, hydrogen is always combined with other elements in chemical **compounds**.

Hydrogen compounds are all around us in the natural world. They are found in coal, oil, natural gas, and animal and plant materials. For example, natural gas contains **methane**, which is a compound of hydrogen and carbon. One molecule of methane has one carbon (C) atom and four hydrogen (H) atoms. The chemical term for methane is CH_4. In addition, 72 percent of the surface of Earth is covered with a very common hydrogen compound—water! (The word *hydrogen* comes from

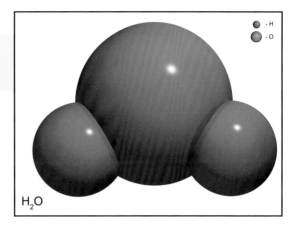

A water molecule is made up of two hydrogen atoms and one oxygen atom.

H_2O

two Greek words: *hydro*, which means "water," and *genes*, which means "to form.") One molecule of water has two hydrogen (H) atoms and one oxygen (O) atom. The chemical term for water is H_2O.

You may have heard of a substance called hydrogen peroxide. You may have used it to disinfect (clean) a cut or scrape. You most certainly have heard of table sugar. Both hydrogen

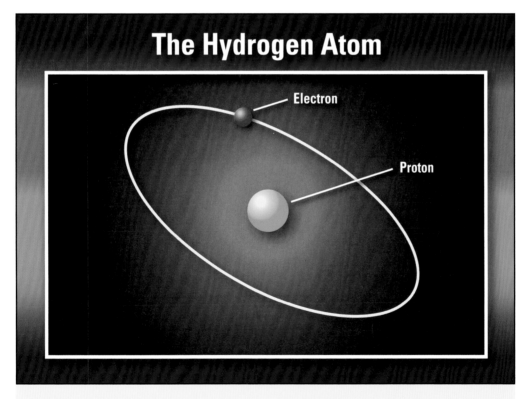

The Hydrogen Atom

Electron

Proton

Hydrogen is the simplest element in the world. A hydrogen atom consists of just one proton and one electron.

peroxide and table sugar are hydrogen compounds. Other common hydrogen compounds include ammonia, hydrochloric acid, and just about every chemical compound found in the human body.

Getting the Hydrogen out of Hydrogen Compounds

The fact that hydrogen is found in so many places makes it very promising as a source from which to make hydrogen fuel. In order for hydrogen to be used as a fuel, however, it must first be separated from the other elements in a compound. This can be done in a number of ways using energy from heat, pressure, electricity, or light.

Remember that even though hydrogen fuel is a good source of energy, it takes a great deal of energy to get the hydrogen out of a hydrogen compound. Also, the best hydrogen fuel is the purest. This means that fuel that is almost all hydrogen is better than fuel that has a lot of hydrogen but also might have

	Compound Name	Elements in the Compound	Common Uses
Common Hydrogen Compounds	Ammonia	nitrogen and hydrogen (NH_3)	Production of agricultural fertilizers, cleaning materials.
	Hydrochloric acid	hydrogen and chlorine (HCl)	Fertilizers, photographic developing liquid, PVC (a type of plastic). HCl is made in the human stomach and helps you digest food.
	Table sugar	carbon, hydrogen, and oxygen ($C_{12}H_{22}O_{11}$)	Sweetener, used in cooking and baking.
	Hydrogen peroxide	hydrogen and oxygen (H_2O_2)	Disinfectant (kills germs), used in a variety of products such as mouthwash, cosmetics, and household cleaners.

some other chemicals in it. The steps needed to get as pure a hydrogen fuel as possible all require some type of energy input. In the end, producing hydrogen fuel makes sense only if the amount of energy you put into making it is far less than the amount of energy you get out of the hydrogen fuel when it is used.

Each of the major processes that are now being used or considered to produce hydrogen that will be used in hydrogen fuel have both benefits and downsides. All of the processes have an energy cost—but in the end, the amount of energy provided by the hydrogen fuel is far in excess of the cost in energy to produce it.

Did You Know?

How Much Hydrogen Is Needed?

According to the U.S. Department of Energy, once hydrogen has become established as an energy carrier, the United States would need about 40 million tons (36.3 million metric tons) of hydrogen per year to provide enough electricity for 25 million homes and enough fuel for 100 million vehicles.

Hydrogen from High-Temperature Steam

Natural gas provides about 23 percent of the energy used in the United States. The natural gas is found in oil deposits, coal beds, and even a type of rock called oil shale. Natural gas is made almost entirely of the chemical methane.

Natural gas can also be used to make hydrogen fuel. About 95 percent of the hydrogen produced today in the United States is made through a process called **steam-methane reforming**. During this process, the methane that is in natural gas reacts

Most of the hydrogen used today is produced in large plants by the process of steam-methane reforming of natural gas.

chemically with extremely hot steam. The steam is between about 1290°F and 1830°F (700°C and 1000°C). A **chemical reaction** takes place that produces a gas that is a mixture of hydrogen and the gas carbon monoxide. The carbon monoxide then has a chemical reaction with the steam to produce a mixture of the gases hydrogen and carbon dioxide.

Steam-methane reforming is considered an efficient way to get hydrogen from a hydrogen compound. This process has been used by the oil refinery and chemical industries for many years. Currently, there is a plentiful supply of natural gas in the United States and Canada (although that may not be true in the future). This also means a plentiful supply of methane. The **pipelines** needed to deliver the natural gas to processing plants are already in place. This saves time and money because many new delivery structures do not have to be built.

Also, steam-methane reforming is about 65 to 75 percent energy efficient, which is considered a high percentage. "Energy efficiency" is defined as the amount of useful energy you get from a system. In other words, even though it takes energy to make hydrogen fuel, it does not take so much energy that it is not worth doing in the first place. In addition, the United States has at least a 60-year supply of natural gas—and possibly much more—so natural gas is a good short-term resource from which to make hydrogen fuel while work goes on to improve other methods of getting the fuel.

An important disadvantage to using steam-methane reforming is that it is expensive to set up and take care of the factories needed. The process uses expensive equipment that must be kept in top running condition at all times. In addition, something must be done to prevent the carbon dioxide that is produced during the process from entering the atmosphere.

Hydrogen from Electrolysis

The process called **electrolysis** uses an electric current in water to cause a chemical reaction. This reaction splits the water molecules into hydrogen and oxygen. The process needs energy—in the form of electricity—to make the hydrogen fuel. The electricity

During electrolysis, an electric current causes water molecules to separate into hydrogen and oxygen.

does not have to come from a fossil fuel source. Instead, it can come from renewable resources such as wind and the Sun. This would provide a never-ending supply of electrical energy to drive the electrolysis that produces hydrogen fuel.

A great deal of Earth's surface—72 percent—is covered by water. The U.S. Navy estimates that there are 361.2 *quintillion* gallons of water just in the world's oceans. In the United States, one quintillion is defined as the number 1 followed by 18 zeroes. So, there is a great deal of water. If the electricity to run the electrolysis process comes from renewable sources, electrolysis can be a very efficient way to produce hydrogen fuel. Currently, it is estimated that this type of process can be 80 to 85 percent efficient. Many believe that electrolysis can be the most efficient means of producing hydrogen fuel over the long term. Today, however, electrolysis is too expensive to be practical for everyday use. In addition, if the electricity used in the process comes from fossil fuel power plants, harmful levels of carbon dioxide and other gases are produced.

Coal Gasification

Coal can be changed into different gases through **gasification**, which is a series of chemical reactions that rely on heat, pressure, and steam. These gases are called **synthesis gas**, or syngas. Syngas is a type of middle point in the hydrogen gas production process. The synthesis gas is a mixture of hydrogen and carbon monoxide. When this gas reacts with steam, it produces even more hydrogen. It also produces carbon dioxide. At this point, the hydrogen can be separated out to produce pure hydrogen that can be used as fuel. The carbon dioxide, however, is a waste product.

Did You Know?
Carbon Capture and Sequestration

Producing hydrogen fuel through gasification also produces carbon dioxide, which contributes to global warming. Scientists and engineers are looking at a process called carbon capture and sequestration, or CCS, to remove excess carbon dioxide from the atmosphere. ("Sequestration" means separation or removal.) CCS is also used to prevent carbon dioxide from getting into the air in the first place.

CCS uses different chemical reactions to capture carbon dioxide. The captured gas is then safely stored in such places as empty oil and gas reservoirs deep inside Earth. (A reservoir is a chamber in which something can be stored.) Storing the carbon dioxide gas so that it cannot cause harm would allow people to use gasification to make hydrogen fuel in a safe way. Currently, CCS is still in the development stages. It is a very expensive process. Scientists are exploring different technologies to make CCS more affordable.

Since coal is a nonrenewable resource, some people wonder why making hydrogen fuel through gasification would be a good thing. Currently, the United States has about a 130-year supply of coal that could be used, which is enough to make the gasification process practical. A big disadvantage, though, is that coal gasification produces carbon dioxide (which can have harmful effects) along with hydrogen.

Even though coal is used in one type of gasification, it turns out that the gasification process to make hydrogen

Did You Know?

Hydrogen on Demand

Is there any way that hydrogen fuel could be easily made in small amounts as it is needed? Jerry Woodall, a professor at Purdue University in Indiana, thinks he might have a way. Woodall discovered that hydrogen is produced when water is added to an **alloy** (a mixture of two or more metals) of aluminum and gallium. The water is added to a tank containing pellets of the alloy. The alloy, which has a strong reaction to the oxygen in the water, splits the water molecules, releasing hydrogen. The hydrogen could then be fed directly into an engine—such as a car engine—where it would act like gasoline. Only the hydrogen that is needed right away would be made. The process is still in the experimental stages, but Woodall and his students are working on making it a practical method to produce hydrogen fuel.

fuel is more efficient than just burning coal. More energy is produced through gasification than is produced in a traditional coal-burning power plant that makes electricity. The energy in the form of hydrogen fuel could be used to generate far more electricity than the coal from which the hydrogen fuel was made. Scientists believe that this benefit outweighs the downside of creating carbon dioxide. In addition, scientists are looking at different processes to reduce the threat that carbon dioxide poses. One of these processes involves taking the

A biomass gasification plant in Hawaii.

carbon dioxide out during the gasification process and storing it where it will not do any harm.

Biomass Gasification

The renewable energy resource **biomass** also can be used in a gasification process to produce hydrogen fuel. Biomass includes organic materials such as wheat straw, animal wastes, forest residues, and special crops like switchgrass or willow trees that are grown to be used as energy sources.

The actual gasification process is similar to that used for coal. One difference is that biomass is more difficult to gasify than coal. It also produces extra waste gases such as carbon dioxide that must be removed. One main benefit, though, is that biomass, unlike coal, will never run out. Another benefit is that many sources of biomass materials are plants. Plants take carbon dioxide out of the atmosphere (during the process of **photosynthesis**) as they grow. This makes up a great deal for the carbon dioxide and other gases that are released into the atmosphere during gasification. In fact, the amount of carbon dioxide taken out of the atmosphere almost equals the amount that is released.

CHAPTER 3

Hydrogen Fuel Cells

So far, hydrogen fuel has most commonly been used in two ways. One way is as powerful rocket fuel. The second way is with a regular gasoline-powered engine as you find in automobiles. (These engines are called internal-combustion engines.) Today, scientists are looking at using hydrogen fuel in exciting new ways, such as in a **device** called a **fuel cell**. Scientists predict that fuel cells could be used in everything from transportation vehicles to cell phones. Many engineers and scientists believe that fuel cells will be in common use as soon as 2020.

Converting Energy

A fuel cell is basically an energy conversion device. This means that it takes one type of energy and changes it to another type of energy. Fuel cells use hydrogen and oxygen to cause a chemical reaction. The chemical reaction produces water and, with it, electricity.

Fuel cells work in a way that is similar to the batteries you might use for portable music players or flashlights. A battery is a sealed container with chemicals inside. The chemicals react with each other and produce **electrons**. These are particles in an atom that have a negative charge. When you use a battery in something like a portable music player, the electrons travel as electricity from one part of the battery through the music

player, then back to the battery again. The electrons follow a **circuit** (a loop). The result? You hear music!

The flow of electrons in and out of a battery continues as long as the chemical reaction takes place and the electrons travel through a device (like the music player described above) or a wire. There is a limited amount of chemicals inside the battery, and as the reactions occur, the chemicals are used up or changed. This is why a battery can "go dead." At some point, it runs out of the chemicals that react with each other. A fuel cell, though, uses a supply of chemicals that comes from outside the cell. This means that the supply can be controlled so that the chemicals needed for the reaction never run out. The chemicals that fuel cells use are hydrogen and oxygen.

A Typical Fuel Cell

Every fuel cell has two **electrodes**. An electrode is a terminal, or place, where an electrical current is conducted. An electrode can have either a positive or a negative charge. The chemical reactions in a fuel cell take place at the electrodes. The electrodes are good conductors of electricity.

Every fuel cell also uses some type of **electrolyte**. An electrolyte is a material that carries electrically charged

SIR WILLIAM GROVE

Sir William Grove was born in Wales in 1811. He became a professor of physics at the London Institution in England. He experimented with different types of batteries. One of these, called a nitric acid cell battery, was used by the U.S. telegraph industry in the middle of the nineteenth century. Grove took his research further, though. He knew that sending an electrical current through water would split water molecules into hydrogen and oxygen atoms. He wondered what would happen if the process was reversed. Grove combined hydrogen and oxygen gases in the presence of an electrical current. The result? A "gas battery" that created electricity and water. This was the first fuel cell ever made. Because of his achievement, Grove is called the "Father of the Fuel Cell." Grove died in London in 1896.

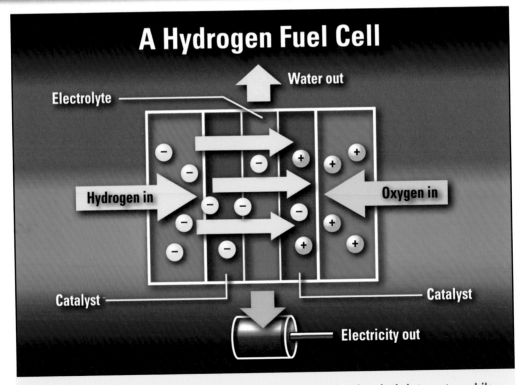

Hydrogen and oxygen flow into a fuel cell, which converts the chemicals into water, while also producing electricity.

particles from one electrode to the other. Electrolytes can be solids, liquids, or pastes. All fuel cells also have a special material called a **catalyst**. The catalyst acts to speed up the chemical reactions in the fuel cell. Some fuel cells use metals such as platinum, nickel, or iron as electrodes or in the catalyst.

Creating a Chemical Reaction

In a hydrogen fuel cell, hydrogen and oxygen are needed for the reactions that will create the flow of electrons that is electricity. This is how it works. Hydrogen gas from a tank is run through a tube or pipe into the fuel cell at one of two electrodes. A chemical reaction causes the hydrogen atoms to lose electrons. These hydrogen atoms are now called **ions**. They are atoms that carry a positive charge. The loose electrons that left the original hydrogen atoms flow along a wire out of the fuel cell as part of an electrical circuit. They produce the electricity.

Did You Know?
Outer Space Water

NASA has long used liquid hydrogen to fuel space rockets. Now NASA also uses fuel cells within the space shuttle cabin to provide electrical power to the shuttle's instruments. The water that is created in the fuel cell is then used as drinking water by the crew.

Workers take apart a fuel cell that has been removed from the space shuttle.

The electrical current then returns to the fuel cell, completing the electrical circuit. When the electrons return to the fuel cell, they come into contact with outside air that has been pulled into the fuel cell at the second electrode. This air contains oxygen. The oxygen that has been pulled in combines with the loose electrons. The oxygen also combines with the positively charged hydrogen ions that have traveled from the other electrode. Hydrogen and oxygen combine to form water, which drains from the fuel cell.

Meanwhile, more hydrogen and oxygen go into the fuel cell, and the process is repeated over and over again. The result? Electricity! As long as there is a supply of hydrogen and oxygen, a fuel cell can keep on producing electricity.

How Are Fuel Cells Used?

How many things can you think of that use electricity? There are big things, of course, like the refrigerator, television set, and computer in your house. Your house probably gets its electricity from a power plant that burns fossil fuels, but fuel cell stacks could also be used to produce this electricity. They

Did You Know?

Fuel Cell Stacks

Some huge fuel cells produce a great deal of electricity. Usually, though, the chemical reaction in fuel cells produces only a small amount of electricity—about 0.7 volts. Compare this to a regular C size battery that you might use in a toy or flashlight. A C battery produces 1.5 volts. Scientists have learned that they can join together, or "stack," fuel cells. This increases the total amount of voltage that a set of fuel cells can produce.

might be used in remote areas where it is difficult to deliver electricity over power lines.

Fuel cells can also be used for other purposes. Think about the energy used by a car or other transportation vehicles. Fuel cells could be an excellent source of electrical energy for the cars and buses of the future. In fact, some researchers think that if hydrogen fuel cell–powered vehicles become common, they will cost less than half of what gasoline powered-vehicles cost today. Hydrogen fuel cell vehicles will also be easier to take care of because there will be fewer parts to repair or replace.

As of 2009, there were only a few hundred hydrogen-fueled vehicles in the United States. (In contrast, there were many more alternative-fueled vehicles of other types.) Very few of the

Did You Know?
Home-Made Fuel Cells

Some people are buying kits that enable them to make their own electricity using one or more fuel cells. Most of the kits include a small solar panel that converts the Sun's energy into electricity. The electricity is used to power a device that makes hydrogen gas, such as a machine that splits water into hydrogen and oxygen gases. The gases are stored in small containers that are then used in a fuel cell to make even more electricity. People use this electricity to power things such as emergency flashlights, cell phones, and radios. Although it sounds complicated, making electricity with fuel cell kits is actually quite easy and can be a lot of fun.

hydrogen-fueled vehicles burned hydrogen like gasoline is burned. Most of them were buses or cars that used fuel cells to provide the electricity to run electric motors that powered the vehicles.

Wal-Mart has purchased hydrogen fuel cell–powered forklifts for its main warehouse. In addition, the U.S. Postal Service has some vehicles that use hydrogen fuel cells. Fuel cell vehicles are also being used in other countries. In 2009,

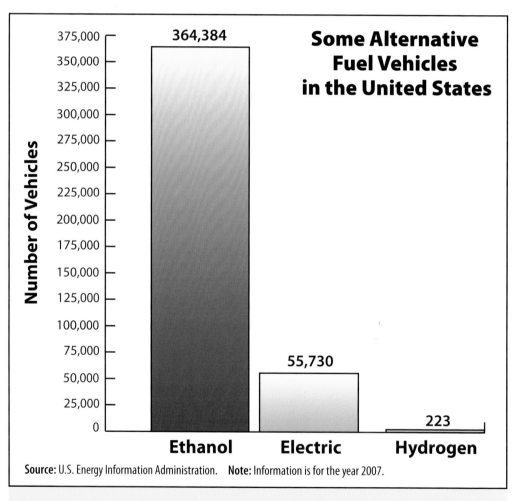

Some Alternative Fuel Vehicles in the United States

Source: U.S. Energy Information Administration.   Note: Information is for the year 2007.

In comparison to other types of vehicles that use alternative fuels, there are very few vehicles that run on hydrogen.

Hydrogen-powered bicycles can go as fast as 15 miles (24 kilometers) per hour.

the city of Sao Paolo, Brazil, introduced the first hydrogen fuel–powered public transportation bus in South America. Similar buses are also in use in parts of Europe, such as the city of Rotterdam in the Netherlands.

Bicycles powered by hydrogen fuel cells have been sold in parts of Asia since 2007. In China, only about 2 percent of the population of more than 1.3 billion people owns a car. Even though car ownership in China is growing, bicycles will still be an important mode of transportation there. Electric bicycles powered with hydrogen fuel cells can go as fast as 15 miles (24 kilometers) per hour. That may not sound very fast, but it is quick in a crowded city. In addition, the hydrogen fuel cell provides power for the bicycle for a great distance of about 185 miles (300 kilometers) before needing to "refuel" on hydrogen.

This Godzilla robot runs on an experimental battery that uses a hydrogen fuel cell.

CHAPTER 4

Challenges in Using Hydrogen Fuel

Hydrogen fuel is made from the most plentiful element in the universe. The actual chemical reaction that forms the fuel results in zero toxic waste. The only "waste" that is made is water, from which even more hydrogen fuel can be made. This is great news for the environment because it helps to limit the amount of carbon dioxide in the atmosphere. Looking at all these facts, it would seem that there could not possibly be a downside to using hydrogen fuel—but there are drawbacks.

The Expense of Making Hydrogen Fuel

It is expensive to produce hydrogen fuel. Even though hydrogen itself is plentiful, it is found in compounds that must be broken apart to release the hydrogen. Each of the processes used today to make hydrogen—such as electrolysis and steam-methane reforming—requires some type of energy. That energy costs money, whether it is for electricity to split apart water molecules or for heat and pressure to break apart a methane molecule. Also, the energy being used to produce the hydrogen fuel has a cost in terms of harmful byproducts that might be produced as well. Currently, it costs more to produce hydrogen fuel than it does to produce fuels such as coal, oil, and natural gas. The high cost of producing hydrogen fuel means that there probably will not be large hydrogen power plants in the near

Since hydrogen can catch on fire, tanks of hydrogen must be kept in a safe, secure place.

future. That may change as technology to produce hydrogen fuel improves.

Storing and Transporting Hydrogen Fuel

Storing and transporting hydrogen fuel also poses challenges. Hydrogen can be stored in a number of ways. It can be stored as a gas, a liquid, or even as part of a chemical compound. Since hydrogen is a gas at room temperature, it is easiest to store it in special tanks called compressed gas cylinders. These are similar to the cylinders you might see at filling stations that refill **propane** gas tanks.

Small amounts of hydrogen gas to be used in vehicles could be produced at filling stations. It is more likely, though, that the hydrogen would need to be produced at larger facilities and somehow transported to filling stations. It would not be practical, however, for trucks to carry massive tanks of hydrogen gas to filling stations, so another method would be needed. The hydrogen gas could be sent through pipelines.

In Germany, there is a large facility that makes hydrogen gas. The gas is then moved through a network of pipes that run about 50 miles (80 kilometers). In the United States, there are about 700 miles (1,125 kilometers) of hydrogen gas pipelines already in place. They are found in just a few regions, mainly where hydrogen is being used in chemical plants and oil refineries in Illinois, California, and along the coast of the Gulf of Mexico. This may sound like plenty of pipeline, but it is really very little compared to the more than one million miles (1.6 million kilometers) of pipeline that transport natural gas.

A large storage tank for liquid hydrogen.

Did You Know?

Hydrogen Fuel Safety

Scientists and engineers are making sure that hydrogen fuel will be safe to use. Hydrogen gas is very flammable—in other words, it easily catches fire. It is really no more flammable, however, than gasoline, which people have used safely for many years. As with gasoline, the first step to safe use of hydrogen fuel is to make sure that there are no leaks in the storage tanks. Scientists are testing different materials for these tanks and believe that hydrogen fuel can be safely stored.

There are very few hydrogen fuel filling stations in the United States today. When these stations are built, however, they will look very similar to today's gas stations. The new filling stations will also have the same safety rules:

- Turn off the vehicle when refueling.
- Do not smoke.
- Do not light a match.
- Do not use cell phones or anything else that can create even a small electrical spark that might cause the fuel to catch on fire.

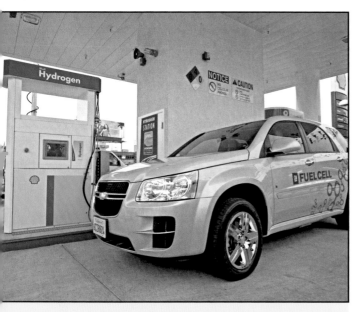

A hydrogen filling station in California.

For hydrogen fuel to be practical for everyday use, the United States would need to add many thousands of miles of new pipeline. This would probably cost millions and millions of dollars to build.

Hydrogen can also be transported in other ways, but they are even more expensive than via pipeline. Compressed

Did You Know?

Filling Stations in Your Garage

What if you had a hydrogen-fueled car but did not have a place to fill it? One possible solution would be a hydrogen fuel filling station in your own garage. Some automobile manufacturers have looked into developing hydrogen generators that people could keep at home. These generators would be about the size of a refrigerator. Having such a generator would let people refill their cars right at home without worrying about trying to find hydrogen filling stations.

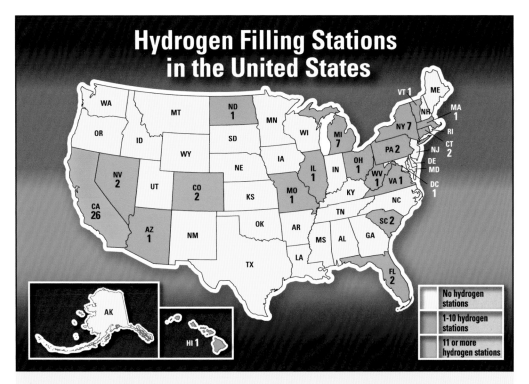

Hydrogen Filling Stations in the United States

VT 1
ME
WA
MT
ND 1
MN
NH
MA 1
OR
ID
SD
WI
MI 7
NY 7
RI
WY
IA
OH 1
PA 2
NJ
CT 2
NV 2
UT
CO 2
NE
IL 1
IN
WV 1
VA 1
DE
MD
CA 26
KS
MO 1
KY
DC 1
NC
AZ 1
NM
OK
AR
TN
SC 2
MS
AL
GA
TX
LA
FL 2

AK

HI 1

No hydrogen stations

1-10 hydrogen stations

11 or more hydrogen stations

As of December 2009, there were 63 hydrogen filling stations in the United States. Many of them are located in California.

hydrogen gas can be placed in special trailers and shipped by truck, train, or ship. This is usually done for distances of less than 200 miles (320 kilometers). Hydrogen can also be specially treated so that, in liquid form, it can be transported by truck, train, or ship. The process to change the gas to a liquid is expensive, though.

The people manufacturing the hydrogen fuel, building the pipelines, and otherwise arranging for transporting the fuel want to be sure that there will be enough hydrogen-fuel vehicles on the road to make the costs worthwhile. From the other view, vehicle manufacturers want to be sure that the hydrogen fuel will be easily available before they spend the money to produce fleets of hydrogen-fueled cars and buses.

CHAPTER 5

The Future of Hydrogen Fuel

One of the challenges for hydrogen fuel is the way it is produced. If it could be produced without using nonrenewable energy sources, it would be seen as more practical. Researchers are working on some promising new technologies with hydrogen fuel.

New Ways of Producing Hydrogen

Researchers believe that, in the future, hydrogen will probably mostly be produced from water. Devices that generate electricity through wind or solar power will likely create the electrical current needed to split water molecules into hydrogen and oxygen atoms. Hydrogen will probably also be produced using a special type of **algae**. Researchers have discovered ways to cause the algae to produce hydrogen for a long period of time. This natural biological reaction can be controlled in what are called algae farms, where hydrogen for fuel cells can be produced at a cost that is far less than the cost of the electrolysis process used today.

Hydrogen Fuel Cell Electricity

There are some exciting ways in which electricity produced through hydrogen fuel might be used. How about a cell phone or MP3 player with a tiny fuel cell in it that provides electricity? How about a laptop powered by a fuel cell that will give you

hours and hours of use?
Miniature fuel cells could
power everything from
watches to hearing aids.

Hydrogen fuel cell
power packs for television
cameras are already being
tested in the United States
and Europe. Television
cameras usually run on
batteries, which eventually
run out of power. The fuel
cell system, though, could
produce almost continuous
electricity. A two-pound
(one-kilogram) hydrogen
canister would allow the
camera to run for up to four
or five hours. In contrast,
a regular rechargeable battery powers the camera for only two
hours before the battery needs to be changed or recharged.

A system for producing hydrogen from algae.

Emergency hydrogen fuel cells could also be used as backup
power in a home during an electrical outage. The fuel cell
would provide enough electricity for hours to power telephones,
radios, and emergency lights. This would be of great use to
firefighters, police, and emergency response teams of all kinds.

Fuel Cells in the Air

Commercial aircraft produce a great deal of pollution when
they burn fuel while flying. In July 2009, Germany tested

the first piloted aircraft that could get into the air using only the power from fuel cells. Absolutely no carbon dioxide was put into the atmosphere. This test plane was a glider, which

Did You Know?
Jobs in the Fuel Cell Industry

Hydrogen fuel cells look likely to be a significant part of the future of technology. According to the U.S. Department of Energy, 675,000 new jobs could be generated in the industry over the next 25 years. Jobs in the fuel cell industry range from electrochemical engineers to people who build and maintain fuel cell systems. If you have an interest in physics or chemistry, jobs in those areas would include research to explain why one catalyst in a fuel cell might be better than another. For now, an interest in math and physical science is the first step to a future job working with fuel cells.

A worker in a Massachusetts plant assembles part of a fuel cell stack.

A hydrogen-powered plane took to the air in Germany in 2009.

means it does not use a motor while in the air. Some day, fuel cell technology may be used to power bigger planes with engines that can carry hundreds of passengers.

Even though there are many challenges to meet, hydrogen fuel presents an excellent choice as an energy resource for the future. As of 2008, more than 40 U.S. states had projects under way, in the U.S. Department of Energy's Hydrogen Program, focusing on hydrogen and fuel cell research and development. Researchers believe that hydrogen is one of the cleanest fuels available. This is very important in a world that needs clean sources of power.

A scientist checks on a device for producing hydrogen using sunlight and water.

Did You Know?

A Hydrogen Fuel
Time Line

1766—British scientist Henry Cavendish identifies hydrogen as a distinct element.

1783—The first hydrogen balloon is launched in France.

1800—British scientists William Nicholson and Sir Anthony Carlisle learn that applying an electric current to water produces oxygen and hydrogen gases.

1838—Swiss-German chemist Christian Friedrich Schönbein discovers that hydrogen and oxygen gases can be combined in a way to produce water and electricity.

1843—British scientist Sir William Grove—later called the "Father of the Fuel Cell"—creates a "gas battery," which is basically a fuel cell.

1920s—German engineer Rudolph Erren converts a standard internal-combustion engine to use hydrogen or hydrogen mixtures.

1959—Professor Francis T. Bacon of Cambridge University in England builds the first hydrogen-air fuel cell, which powers a welding machine.

1959—Harry Karl Ihrig, an engineer at the Allis-Chalmers Manufacturing Company in the United States, demonstrates the first vehicle powered by a fuel cell—a 20-horsepower farm tractor.

1972—A 1972 Ford Gremlin internal-combustion engine is modified by students at the University of California at Los Angeles to run on hydrogen. The modified Gremlin wins first prize in a competition for the vehicle with the lowest tailpipe emissions.

1988—Scientists in the Soviet Union successfully convert a 164-passenger commercial jet to fly with one of the jet's three engines powered by liquid hydrogen. Even though the flight lasts only 21 minutes, it opens the door to the use of liquid hydrogen in jet engines.

1990—The world's first solar-powered production plant to produce hydrogen opens in southern Germany.

1994—The Daimler Benz Motor Company in Germany demonstrates its first fuel cell vehicle.

2003—President George W. Bush announces the beginning of a $1.2 billion hydrogen fuel initiative to pursue hydrogen fuel technology.

2004—Germany tests the world's first fuel cell–powered submarine in deep water.

2008—More than 40 U.S. states have hydrogen research and development projects under way, in the U.S. Department of Energy's Hydrogen Program.

acid rain: Rain, snow, fog, or mist that contains acid substances and damages the environment.

algae: Life forms that resemble plants and that usually grow in water.

alloy: A mixture of two or more metals.

atmosphere: The envelope of air that surrounds the planet.

atom: The smallest part of an element that has the properties of that element.

biomass: Plants and animal wastes that can be used as fuel.

carbon dioxide: A gas formed when fossil fuels are burned; also written as CO_2.

catalyst: A substance that speeds up a chemical reaction.

chemical reaction: A process that changes the molecules of substances by moving atoms around.

circuit: A path followed by an electrical current.

compound: A substance that is formed when two or more elements unite.

device: Something that does some action.

electrode: A terminal where an electric current flows in or out.

electrolysis: The use of an electric current to break down a chemical compound into its components.

electrolyte: A solution of chemicals that conducts electricity.

electron: A small, negatively charged particle in an atom.

element: A basic chemical substance that cannot be divided into simpler substances.

fossil fuels: Fuels, such as coal, natural gas, or oil, that were formed underground over millions of years from the remains of prehistoric plants and animals. Such fuels are not renewable.

fuel cell: A device that uses a reaction between two substances, such as hydrogen and oxygen, to make electricity.

gasification: The process of changing a liquid or solid into a gas.

global warming: The gradual warming of Earth's atmosphere and surface, caused by the buildup of carbon dioxide and other greenhouse gases that trap heat.

hydrogen fuel: Fuel that uses hydrogen gas or liquid as an energy carrier.

ion: An atomic particle that has a charge.

mass: The amount of physical matter in an object.

methane: A gas used as a fuel that is the main ingredient in natural gas. It is a compound of hydrogen and carbon.

nonrenewable: A resource of which there is only a certain amount. Sources such as coal, natural gas, and oil are nonrenewable.

photosynthesis: The process by which plants use energy from the Sun to turn water and carbon dioxide into food; they then give off oxygen.

pipeline: A series of pipes that are used to transport water, gas, or oil from one location to another over long distances.

power plant: A place for the production of electric power, also sometimes called a "power station."

propane: A type of gas that may be used as a fuel.

prototype: The first version of an invention, used to test out the invention.

refined: Made more pure through a chemical process.

renewable: A resource that never gets used up. Energy sources such as sunlight, wind, and biofuels are renewable; sources such as coal, natural gas, and oil are nonrenewable.

steam-methane reforming: The most common method to get hydrogen out of methane gas, in which the methane reacts chemically with extremely hot steam.

synthesis gas: Also called syngas, a mixture of hydrogen and carbon monoxide produced during the middle of the coal gasification process. When this gas reacts with steam, it produces even more hydrogen.

Read these books:

Hayhurst, Chris. *Hydrogen Power for the Future: New Ways of Turning Fuel Cells into Energy*. New York: Rosen, 2003.

Lew, Kristi. *Goodbye, Gasoline: The Science of Fuel Cells*. Minneapolis: Compass Point Books, 2009.

Lippman, David. *Energy from Hydrogen*. Ann Arbor, Michigan: Cherry Lake, 2008.

Morgan, Sally. *From Windmills to Hydrogen Fuel Cells*. Chicago: Heinemann, 2008.

Solway, Andrew. *Hydrogen Fuel*. Pleasantville, New York: Gareth Stevens, 2008.

Walker, Niki. *Hydrogen: Running on Water*. New York: Crabtree, 2007.

Look up these Web sites:

Collecting the History of Fuel Cells
http://americanhistory.si.edu/fuelcells

EIA Energy Kids Page: Hydrogen
http://tonto.eia.doe.gov/kids/energy.cfm?page=hydrogen_home-basics

How Fuel Cells Work
http://auto.howstuffworks.com/fuel-efficiency/alternative-fuels/fuel-cell.htm

H2 and You
http://www.h2andyou.org

The Hydrogen Community
http://www.hydrogensociety.net

Key Internet search terms:

fuel cell, hydrogen, hydrogen fuel

INDEX

The abbreviation *ill.* stands for illustration, and *ills.* stands for illustrations. Page references to illustrations and maps are in *italic* type.

About the Author

Barbara J. Davis has written books on science topics for kids for more than 15 years. She has published books on ecosystems and biomes as well as earth science subjects.